INSTRUMENTS *in* MUSIC

ROCK, POP AND DANCE

Roger Thomas

Heinemann Library
Des Plaines, Illinois

Designed by Susan Clarke
Printed in Hong Kong

02 01 00 99 98
10 9 8 7 6 5 4 3 2 1

Library of Congress Cataloging-in-Publication Data

Thomas, Roger, 1956-
    Rock, pop, and dance / Roger Thomas.
        p.   cm. — (Instruments in music)
    Includes bibliographical references and index.
    Summary: Briefly discusses rock, pop, and dance music and
introduces some of their instruments, including electric guitar,
drum kit, and computer sequencers.
    ISBN 1-57572-645-9 (lib. bdg.)
    1. Musical instruments—Juvenile literature. 2. Rock music—
History and criticism—Juvenile literature. 3. Popular music—
History and criticism—Juvenile literature. 4. Dance music—
History and criticism—Juvenile literature. [1. Musical
instruments. 2. Rock music. 3. Popular music. 4. Dance music.]
    I. Title.   II. Series.
ML460.T425 1998
784.164—dc21

97-49501
CIP
AC MN

Acknowledgements
The Publishers would like to thank the following for permission to reproduce photographs:
Aria, p.21 top, middle; Combi Press, p.9 inset; Trevor Clifford, pp.10, 11 (Dominic Goundar), p.14 (Hertfordshire
County Music Service), pp.6, 8, 9, 13, 20, 28 (The Music Dept.), p.22 (John Myatt Brass and Woodwind), p.12
(Wembley Drum Center), pp.16, 17 (Yamaha-Kemble Music (UK) Ltd); Liz Eddison, pp.26, 27, p.18 (CTS Studios);
Redferns, p.25, pp.4, 15 (Fin Costello), p.23 (Dave Ellis), p.5 (Mick Hutson), p.29 (Roberta Parkin); Trip, p.7 (B.
Gadsby); Yamaha, p.19 (Peter Peck), p.21; Zefa, p.24

Cover photograph: Redferns/Mick Hutson

Our thanks to Betty Root for her comments in the preparation of this book.

Every effort has been made to contact copyright holders of any material reproduced in this book. Any omissions will
be rectified in subsequent printings if notice is given to the Publisher.

Any words appearing in bold, **like this,** are explained in the Glossary.

CONTENTS

Introduction 4

The Electric Guitar 6

The Electric Bass Guitar 8

The Drum Kit 10

The Electronic Drum Kit and Drum Machine 12

Percussion Instruments 14

Keyboards and Electronic Instruments 16

Computers and Sequencers 18

Effects and Sound Processors 20

The Horn Section 22

Singing 24

DJ Equipment 26

Microphones and P.A. Equipment 28

Glossary 30

More Books to Read.. 31

Index 32

INTRODUCTION

Rock music began about forty years ago in the United States. It was a mixture of jazz, blues, gospel, and dance music, played with a lively **beat**. Pop music as we now think of it began about ten years later when this mixture of different music became more popular. Since then many different styles of rock and pop have been played.

This is a typical rock band performing a concert.

A DJ playing dance music

Dance music has always been an important part of pop music. Today, however, it usually means very fast, loud, and exciting music often played by people who mix the music on different records together. They are called DJs, from the words "disc jockey." This book is about the different instruments and pieces of **equipment** used by DJs and rock and pop musicians.

THE ELECTRIC GUITAR

The **electric** guitar is one of the most important instruments in rock and pop music. It was invented because the acoustic guitar was too quiet to be heard in loud bands. The sound of the strings is collected by one or more **pickups** on the guitar. They turn the sound into an electrical **signal**. A **cable** takes the signal to an **amplifier**. The amplifier makes the sound as loud as the player wants.

This electric guitar has six strings. It is connected to an amplifier.

This guitarist is playing an electric guitar.

There are **volume** and **tone** controls on the electric guitar and amplifier. These can change the sound. Electric guitar players can either play tunes using single **notes** (lead guitar) or they can play **chords**.

THE ELECTRIC BASS GUITAR

The **electric** bass guitar plays lower **notes** than the electric guitar. It is used to play a low-pitched part in rock and pop music. It is played through an **amplifier** like an electric guitar. The amplifier can make the sound as loud as the player wants.

This electric bass guitar has a **pickup** and four strings. It is connected to an amplifier.

The electric bass guitar was invented to replace the double bass in rock and roll music. It was easier to carry and to play. The electric bass guitar could also be played more loudly.

The double bass

A bassist usually plays one note at a time.

THE DRUM KIT

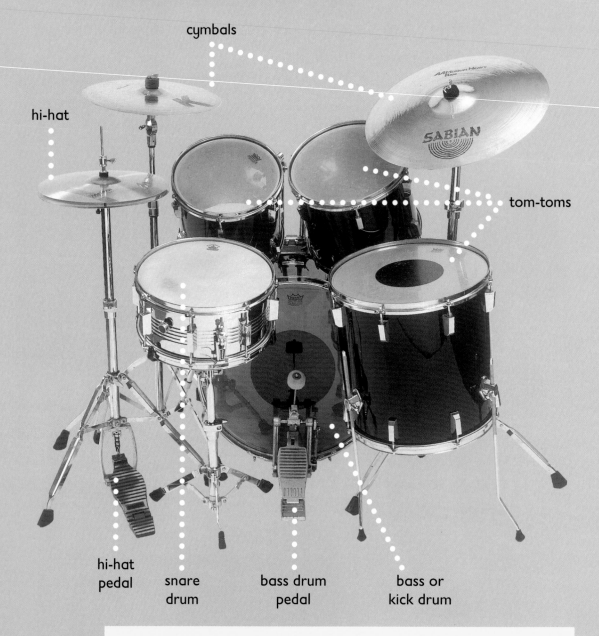

cymbals

hi-hat

tom-toms

hi-hat
pedal

snare
drum

bass drum
pedal

bass or
kick drum

This is a complete drum kit.

Drum kits were first used in jazz and popular music many years ago. They were made up from drums and **percussion** instruments from many different kinds of music. Today they are made as complete kits.

Drummers often use both hands and feet at once.

Most rock and pop bands use a drum kit. The drummer has two important jobs. One is to mark the time of the music. The other is to add extra **beats** and sounds which make the music more interesting. In rock and pop music the drum kit is usually played with hard sticks. Sometimes soft sticks or wire or plastic brushes are also used.

THE ELECTRONIC DRUM KIT AND DRUM MACHINE

Some drummers use **electronic** drum kits. These kits can remember many different sounds. The player can change the sounds easily. The sounds are stored in the drum kit's electronic **memory**. These kits must be played through an **amplifier**.

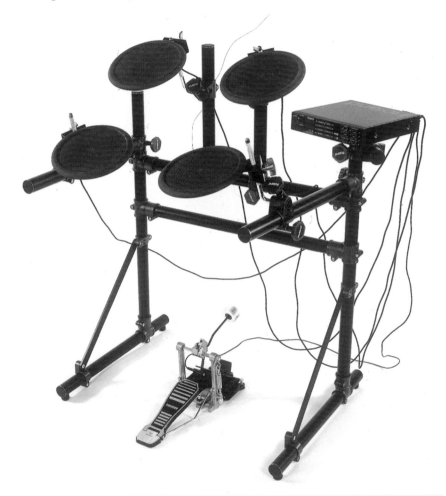

This electronic drum kit can sound like ordinary drums. It can also be made to sound like other instruments. It is usually played with hard sticks.

This electronic drum machine has a memory with drum, cymbal, and percussion sounds in it.

Drum machines are often used in dance music and to make **recordings**. The musician can make the drum machine remember the drum part of a song. The machine will then play the part whenever the musician wants. Drum machines can be made to play very fast or difficult parts. They have to be played through an amplifier or into a **tape recorder** or **hard disk** recorder.

PERCUSSION INSTRUMENTS

Percussion instruments are sometimes used in rock and pop music as well as a drum kit. They add different sounds and **rhythms** to the music. The instruments will often come from many different countries. The person who plays these instruments is called a percussionist.

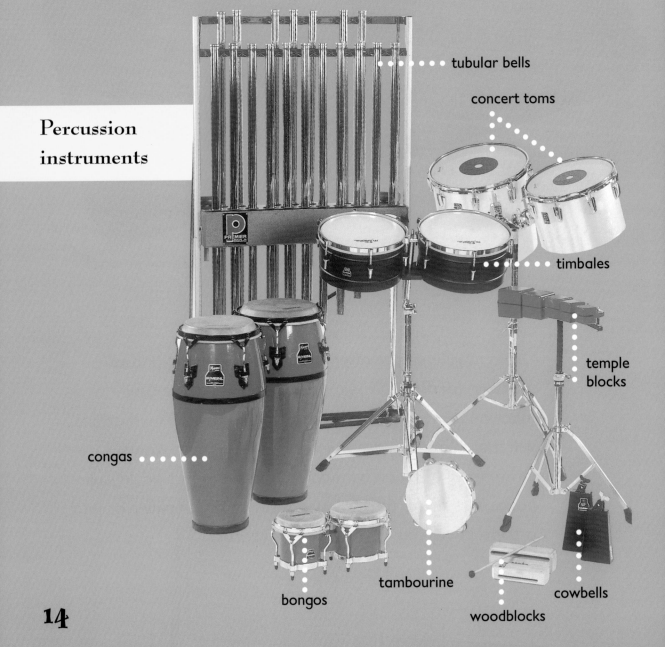

Percussion instruments

tubular bells

concert toms

timbales

temple blocks

congas

bongos

tambourine

woodblocks

cowbells

This percussionist is playing many different percussion instruments.

Different percussion instruments will make different sounds depending on what they are made of. For example, conga and bongo drums are made of wood and have a warm, dry sound. Timbale drums are made of metal and sound much brighter. Many percussion instruments are played with the percussionist's hands. Others are played with hard or soft sticks.

KEYBOARDS AND ELECTRONIC INSTRUMENTS

Electronic instruments like these are very important in rock, pop and dance music. The player can make lots of different sounds with them. They can sound like other instruments or make their own special sounds. The sounds can be changed easily. They must be played through **amplifiers**.

These electronic keyboard instruments, sound modules, and samplers can make hundreds of different sounds

keyboard

sampler

sound module

These are all electronic musical instruments.

Some keyboards have no sounds of their own and can only play the sounds of other electronic instruments. To do this they are linked to the other instruments by **cables**.

Sound modules contain many different sounds. They cannot be played by themselves. Instead they must be controlled by a keyboard or by another electronic instrument.

Samplers can record any sound and turn it into musical **notes**. They cannot be played by themselves either. They must be controlled in the same way as a sound module.

Ordinary pianos are also used in rock and pop music. Sometimes the lead singer also plays the piano.

COMPUTERS AND SEQUENCERS

Computers are often used to help musicians make rock, pop, and dance music. They can make and play sounds. Computers can also remember and play the songs the musicians has put into them. The sounds and songs can easily be changed if the musicians have new ideas. Computers can also record other instruments onto a **hard disk**.

These computers are used for music.

Sequencers have small keys and buttons for putting in sounds, **notes,** and **rhythms.**

A sequencer is a special small computer. It can only be used for music. Sequencers can remember and play songs put into them. Some of them can also make sounds. Sequencers are small and easy to carry, so they can easily be used for **concerts**. They are often used in dance music.

EFFECTS AND SOUND PROCESSORS

Effects and sound processors are used to change the sound of **electric** and **electronic** instruments. Effects pedals are usually used with electric guitars. They can also be used with electric bass guitars. Each processor changes the sound of the instrument in a different way. Some add a "fuzzy" sound to the instrument. Others add "whoosh" or "wah-wah" sounds. There are many other types.

These effects pedals are placed on the floor in front of the musician so she can step on them.

reverberation unit

graphic equalizer

compressor

These sound processors can be used on instruments or on recordings of instruments. They all change the sound in different ways.

A reverberation unit, also called "reverb," makes the sound of the instrument echo. This is often used to make **recordings** sound more like **live music**.

A graphic equalizer changes the **tone** of a sound. It can make the different **notes** played on an instrument sound brighter or softer.

A compressor can make the beginning, middle, and end of a note sound equally loud. This can make the sound of the instrument clearer.

21

THE HORN SECTION

Some rock and pop bands include a group of brass and woodwind players. They are called a horn section, although none of their instruments are really horns! They can make the music sound more powerful and varied.

tenor saxophone

trumpet

trombone

Saxophones, trumpets, and trombones can be used together in rock and pop horn sections.

This horn section has trumpets, a trombone, and a saxophone.

Horn sections are usually added to a rock or pop group which already has guitars, bass, keyboards, drums, and voices. Often there is just one player of each instrument in a horn section but there can be more. Sometimes one of the players will play a **solo** between verses of a song.

SINGING

The lead singer in a rock or pop group sings the main part of the song and is the most important singer in the band. The song may need to be exciting, gentle, happy, sad, or even frightening! Some lead singers play an instrument while they sing.

Here is a lead singer. This job in a rock or pop group is often called "lead vocals."

This is a group of backup singers.

Rock and pop bands will sometimes use extra singers to add other parts to songs. This job is usually called "backup vocals." Back-up vocals can also be sung by the other musicians in the band while they play their instruments.

DJ EQUIPMENT

Dance music DJs can make new music by mixing the music on different records together. The DJ can use controls on the turntable and **mixer** to change the speed and loudness of the records. This makes the music on different records fit together better.

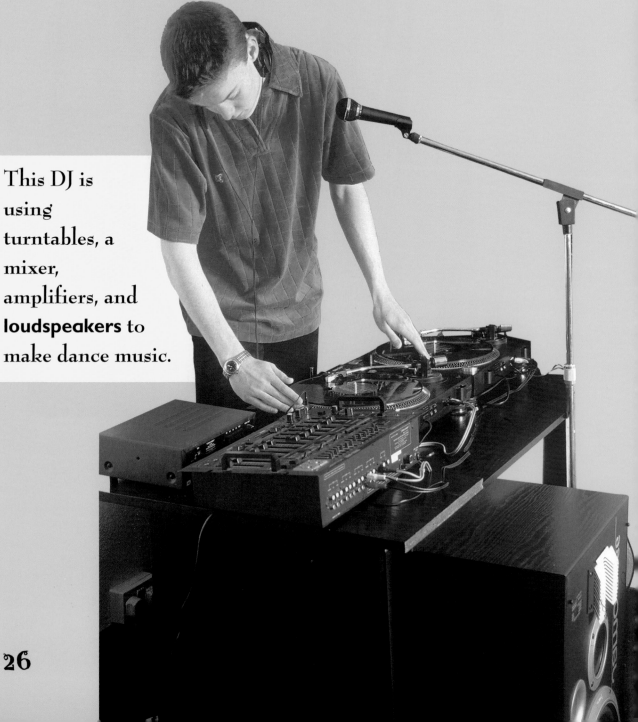

This DJ is using turntables, a mixer, amplifiers, and **loudspeakers** to make dance music.

This is how the sound is collected from a vinyl record.

Dance music can be performed live or made into a new **recording**. DJs usually use **vinyl** records for mixing because it is easy to change the speed. It is also easy to start and stop the music quickly anywhere on the record. A pointed **stylus** fits into the groove on the record. The stylus picks up the music. It is then sent as a **signal** to an **amplifier**.

MICROPHONES AND P.A. EQUIPMENT

Microphones are used to make voices and instruments loud enough to be heard at a **concert** and to put sounds onto **recordings**. In a concert the microphones collect the sound of the voices and instruments and send them through a big **amplifier** and **loudspeakers**. This is called a P.A., or "public address" system.

These microphones and P.A. system can be used for a concert.

These singers are using microphones.

The audience would not be able to hear the singers without microphones because a band's instruments can sound very loud. Rock and pop singers have to learn to use microphones properly. If they are too close to or too far away from the microphone their voices will not be clear.

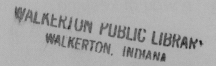

GLOSSARY

amplifier   an electrical device which makes sound louder

beat   one count in musical time

cable   a wire which carries electricity or an electrical signal

chords   several notes played at once

computers   electronic machines which hold and organize information

concert   a performance of live music

electric   a kind of instrument with a quiet sound made louder by an amplifier

electronic   a kind of instrument which creates sound from electrical power

equipment   the instruments, machines and accessories used by a band or DJ

hard disk   a type of computer memory which can also record sound

live music   music which is being played to an audience by the musicians

loudspeakers   boxes which send amplified sound out to an audience

memory   a way of keeping information in computers and other electronic equipment

mixer   a piece of equipment which lets musicians and DJs combine sounds from different instruments or recordings

notes   musical sounds

percussion   instruments played by hitting or tapping

pickups   kinds of microphone for the strings on an electric guitar or bass guitar

recordings   music kept on a tape, a record or in a computer for listening to again

rhythms   the regular patterns of notes in music

signal   a message

solo   one musician playing

stylus   a tiny needle which picks the sound up from vinyl records

tape recorder   a machine which can hold sound on a tape

tone   whether a sound is soft and smooth or hard and bright

vinyl   records made on discs of black plastic with grooves on them which the stylus fits into to collect the sound

volume   the loudness of a sound

MORE BOOKS TO READ

Kallen, Stuart. *Renaissance of Rock: Sounds of America-The Sixties.* Minneapolis, MN: Abdo & Daughters.1989.

Kallen, Stuart. *Retrospective of Rock: The Eighties.* Minneapolis, MN: Abdo & Daughters.1989.

Kallen, Stuart. *Revolution of Rock: The Seventies.* Minneapolis, MN: Abdo & Daughters.1989.

INDEX

amplifier 6–9, 12–13, 16, 26–28
back-up vocals 25
bass drum 10
bongos 14–15

computer 18
concert toms 14
congas 14–15
cymbal 10

DJ 5, 26–27
double bass 9
drum kit 10–11
drum machine 13

effects pedals 20
electric bass guitar 8–9
electric guitar 6–7
electronic drum kit 12

hi-hat 10
horn section 22–23

keyboards 16–17
kick drum 10

lead vocals 24

microphones 28–29

PA equipment 28
piano 17

sampler 17
saxophone 22–23
sequencer 19
singing 24–25
snare drum 10
sound processors 21

tambourine 14
temple blocks 14
timbales 14–15
tom-toms 10
tone control 7
trombone 22–23
trumpet 22–23
tubular bells 14

volume control 7

woodblock 14